On the farm

Nelson

On the farm

Tractor driver, riding high,
In his cab, so warm and dry,
Riding under a cold grey sky,

Rickety-rackety rattle!

Farmer chopping wood for the fire,
See his axe swing higher and higher,
Nearly as high as the tall church spire,

Chop! Chop! Chop!

A dish of corn for the big brown hens,
Pushing, pecking, eight, nine, ten,
Cockerel standing tall in his pen,

Cock-a-doodle-doo!

Cows are coming to the gate,
Supper time has come too late,
Here's one cow who just can't wait,

Workers digging all around,
Digging in the frosty ground,
Digging up carrots
    at ten pence a pound,

Crunch! Crunch! Crunch!

Little girl in the apple tree,
Picking apples for you and me,

I'll have an apple for my tea!

Munch! Munch! Munch!

Old MacDonald

Old Macdonald had a farm
E-I-E-I-O

And on that farm he had some cows
E-I-E-I-O

With a MOO MOO here
And a MOO MOO there
Here a MOO, there a MOO
Everywhere a MOO MOO

Old Macdonald had a farm
E-I-E-I-O

And on that farm he had some sheep
E-I-E-I-O

With a BAA BAA here
And a BAA BAA there
Here a BAA, there a BAA
Everywhere a BAA BAA

Old Macdonald had a farm
E-I-E-I-O

And on that farm he had some pigs
E-I-E-I-O

With an OINK OINK here
And an OINK OINK there
Here an OINK, there an OINK
Everywhere an OINK OINK

Old Macdonald had a farm
E-I-E-I-O

And on that farm he had some ducks
E-I-E-I-O

With a QUACK QUACK here
And a QUACK QUACK there
Here a QUACK, there a QUACK
Everywhere a QUACK QUACK

Old Macdonald had a farm
E - I - E - I - O

Blow, wind, blow!

Blow, wind, blow!

And go, mill, go!

That the miller can grind his corn,

That the baker may take it,
And into bread make it,
And give us a loaf in the morn.

Granny Goat

Eat anything,
  will Granny Goat,
  handkerchiefs,
  the sleeve of your coat,
  sandwiches,
  a ten pound note,
  eat anything,
  will Granny Goat.

Granny Goat
  goes anywhere,
  into the house
  if you're not there,
  follows you round,
  doesn't care,
  Granny Goat
  goes anywhere.

Granny Goat
will not stay
tied up
throughout the day,
chews the rope,
wants to play,
Granny Goat
won't stay ...

anywhere you
want her to,
she would rather be
with *you*!